WATER

Gabrielle Woolfitt

Wayland

Titles in this series
Air
Earth
Fire
Water

TOPIC CHART

	SCIENCE*	ENGLISH	MATHS*	TECHNOLOGY	GEOGRAPHY	HISTORY	PHYSICAL EDUCATION	MUSIC	ART	RELIGIOUS EDUCATION
What is water?	AT 2 L3	✔		✔	✔	✔	✔		✔	✔
Water in the home			AT 2 L4–5		AT 3 L2 AT 2 L4					
Travelling by water	AT 1 L2–4 AT 4 L3–4			AT 1 L2–5 AT 2 L2–5	✔	CSU 1 CSU 6				
Water poems		AT 1 L2–4 AT 2 L2–3						✔		
Water in religion										✔
The water cycle	AT 3 L2, L5	AT 3 L3	AT 1 L3 AT 5 L2		AT 5 L4 AT 1 L2–4					
Seacape									✔	
Water power	AT 4 L3–4			ALL ATS LEVELS 2–5						
Water sports							✔			
Solid, liquid, gas	AT 3 L2–4	AT 2 L3								
Water myths		AT 3 L2–5				AT 2 L2				✔
Dirty water	AT 2 L2–5	AT 2 L2–4			AT 5 L2–5					
Drawing a map	AT 2 L2–4 AT 3 L3			ALL ATS LEVELS 2–5						
Making a water-clock			AT 1 L3 AT 5 L3	AT 3 L2–3					✔	

KEY CSU = Core Study Unit AT = Attainment Target L = Level *Proposed ATs, October 1991

First published in 1992 by
Wayland (Publishers) Ltd
61 Western Road, Hove
East Sussex BN3 1JD, England

© Copyright 1992 Wayland (Publishers) Ltd

Editor: Cath Senker
Designer: Helen White
Consultant: Tom Collins,
Deputy Headmaster of St. Leonards
CEP School, East Sussex

British Library Cataloguing in Publication Data

Woolfitt, Gabrielle
Water. – (The elements)
I. Title II. Series
553.7

ISBN 0 7502 0355 2

Typeset by White Design
Cover and inside artwork by Maureen Jackson
Printed by G. Canale & C.S.p.A. Turin
Bound in France by A.G.M.

CONTENTS

Words printed in **bold** are explained in the glossary.

WHAT IS WATER?

RIGHT **This girl is up to her neck in water!**

Water is the most important liquid on earth. Every living thing needs water. Plants need water to make their food. People and animals need water to drink and to wash with. Did you know that your body is made up mostly of water?

Water is sometimes very powerful. Floods can wash away houses and people. Water has shaped our valleys and coastlines. Frozen rivers called glaciers cut huge channels out of rock. Rivers gradually wear away the sides of a valley over thousands of years.

Water is a good way of moving around. Rivers and oceans connect all the different parts of the world. People use water to transport things from one place to another. Some animals travel around the world using the seas and rivers.

Water plays a very important part in the weather. Can you imagine never having seen a cloud? Water can seem to be all sorts of colours. Water is good for playing sports. How do you use water in your life?

BELOW **This picture, called *The Man on the Tiller*, was painted in 1892 by a Dutch artist. Do you like the way it shows the sea?**

WATER IN THE HOME

This list shows how much water is used for some everyday activities.

1 flush of the toilet	10 litres
1 bath	70 litres
1 wash in the sink	3 litres
1 washing-machine load	90 litres
1 bowl of washing-up	10 litres

BELOW **How much water do you think is in this bath?**

Four people living in a house use about 500 litres of water a day! Try to work out how much you use in your home every day. If something is not on the list try to guess how much water it would take. A bucket holds 10 litres. Work out how many buckets of water you use at home in a day.

Our water comes out of taps. Water is sucked out of rivers or **aquifers.** It is cleaned and piped to our homes. In many parts of the world, lots of people do not have taps. They pump water from a well in the village, or collect water from the river. People have to carry all the water they need. If the area is very hot and dry, the nearest water could be 10 km from home! The water may not be clean. Children in poor countries often become ill from drinking dirty water.

Carry two buckets of water round the school playground. How long would it take you to collect all the water you use every day?

ABOVE **These children must not let dirty river water into the pots of fresh water they are carrying on their heads.**

TRAVELLING BY WATER

For thousands of years people have built boats and ships. At first, boats were very small and needed human strength to move them. The Vikings rowed hundreds of kilometres to invade northern and western Europe about 1,000 years ago. Ships with sails use wind power. In the 1400s, people from western Europe began to explore the world in sailing ships.

Now we can travel on ferries and hovercraft when we go on holiday. Jamaican bananas, Brazilian coffee and Indian cotton all travel on huge ships. They are carried round the world and sold in countries where people cannot grow those crops. Boats can float in water although they are often very heavy. Some very small things sink. Try this experiment.

Make a collection of objects made from different materials, such as wood, metal and plastic. Which ones do you think will float? Which ones do you think will sink? These are your **predictions.** Now put the objects in a bowl of water. Were your predictions right? Can you see a pattern in your results?

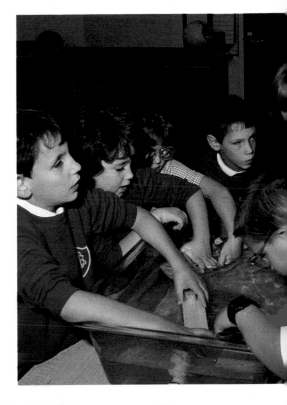

ABOVE **These children are doing an experiment with floating and sinking.**

LEFT **Vikings travelled by ship from Norway, Sweden and Denmark. This ship came from Norway. It had a sail, and oars for rowing as well.**

WATER POEMS

Think of some songs and poems about water. What does each one tell us about water? This poem is all about winter weather in England.

On Monday icy rains poured down
and flooded drains all over town.

Tuesday's gales bashed elm and ash:
dead branches came down with a crash.

On Wednesday bursts of hail and sleet.
No-one walked along our street.

Thursday stood out clear and calm
but the sun was paler than my arm.

Friday's frost that bit your ears
was cold enough to freeze your tears.

Saturday's sky was ghostly grey:
we smashed ice on the lake today.

Christmas Eve was Sunday .... and
snow fell and fell across the land.

by Wes Magee

Write down some words that describe the sound of
water. Now think of some words for the way water
feels to touch. Try to compose a poem about water.
You could make the poem about water in your life.
Do you go swimming? Do you like watching waves on
the beach? How does it feel to be caught in the rain?

LEFT **This is Gene
Kelly in the film
*Singin' in the
Rain*. He certainly
doesn't mind being
wet!**

WATER IN RELIGION

Water is very good for cleaning things. Some religious people wash in special ways. It helps them to feel clean on the inside.

In the Christian religion, people are **baptized.** A priest baptizes the baby with water that has been blessed. Many Christians believe that you must be baptized before you can go to heaven.

Some Christians wait until their children are old enough to understand what baptism means.

BELOW **This Jamaican boy is being baptized by having his whole body put under the water.**

LEFT **Sikh men wear turbans on their heads. The blue turban that this man wears is supposed to show that he treats all people fairly.**

The Golden Temple in Amritsar, India, is a very special place. Sikhs come from all over the world to visit it. The temple stands on an island in the middle of a lake. Sikhs believe the water in the lake is holy. This boy and his father come to bathe in the holy lake every week.

Muslims who practise their religion go to a mosque to pray. There are taps outside the mosque. People take their shoes off and bathe their feet. They go into the mosque barefoot.

THE WATER CYCLE

The water cycle explains how all the water in the world moves from place to place. Follow the arrows and read the labels.

clouds form...

water evaporates from the sea...

Water evaporates from trees

rain falls...

snow falls...

snow melts...

trees absorb water from ground...

water runs into...

...the rivers and streams

The sea contains 97% of all the earth's water...

rivers run into the sea

Water from the sea **evaporates** and forms clouds. Clouds travel over land and then the water falls as rain or snow. The water runs into rivers and streams.

Some clouds are made out of the water from plants. A big forest is like a sponge. When it rains the trees soak up water. The water then evaporates out of the leaves and makes a new cloud. The newly-formed cloud will drop rain on another place.

If we cut down trees less rain will fall. Why do we need rain? What happens when there is not enough rain? Why do people cut down the trees?

How often does it rain where you live? Make a chart of the weather for a month. You must fill it in every day.

LEFT **Trees from this forest are cut into logs which are sold to other countries. If no new trees are planted there will be less rain.**

SEASCAPE

BELOW **This seascape is by a famous Japanese artist called Hokusai. Do you think the people in the boats will survive the storm?**

A seascape is a picture that shows the sea. It is very difficult to make the sea look real in paintings because it is always moving.

You could paint a seascape. First you need to decide which colours to use. The sea is not always blue. It changes colour depending on the weather and the time of day. The sea can look green and grey and black and purple and all the colours in between!

Start by mixing paints together to make some sea colours. When you have made several different shades, try to put them together to look like the sea. Is your sea rough? Is there a storm? Are there any ships? What time of day is it? Try to show these things in your picture.

WATER POWER

ABOVE **This very old water-wheel, called a noria, was used to pump up water to the town of Hama in Syria.**

Water can be very powerful. People have used the power of water for many centuries. Water-wheels were used to provide power for flour mills. The force of the river turns the wheel. A **spindle** from the wheel turns a set of gears. The gears move the machinery that does the work.

Steam Turbine

The steam goes in here.

Most electricity is made in power stations.

Coal or oil is burnt...

It heats up water...

The water becomes very hot and turns into steam...

The steam makes the blades of the turbine go round and round.

Electricity Generator

The steam comes out here.

The steam turbine provides the power for the generator, which produces electricity.

Power Cable

Hydroelectric power is made when water rushes out of **reservoirs**. The moving water turns the **turbines** to make the electricity. Wave power and tidal power can also be used to make electricity.

WATER SPORTS

If you want to be safe near water, you should learn how to swim. Swimming is one of the best kinds of exercise you can take. Swimming uses most of the muscles in your body. This makes your muscles stronger. If you have an injury or a disability you might have **hydrotherapy** in a pool.

ABOVE **This boy is having hydrotherapy.**

You have to work hard if you are going to swim fast. Swimming is an **aerobic exercise**. It is very good for your heart and your breathing. There are four different strokes. Backstroke is the only stroke where you can't see where you are going.

Freestyle, or front crawl, is very fast. Olympic swimmers can swim 100 metres freestyle in 50 seconds! Butterfly is difficult. You have to lift both arms out of the water at the same time. Breaststroke can be very fast, but practise it slowly while you learn.

There are lots of other water sports. Canoeing and rowing are good fun on sunny days. Water polo is a team game that you can play in the pool with your friends.

ABOVE **This woman is swimming freestyle.**
LEFT **This girl is learning how to paddle a canoe.**

SOLID, LIQUID, GAS

Water is a liquid. You can pour water. You cannot pour ice! Ice is a solid. Steam is a gas. It spreads out in the air. Look at the picture opposite. Make a list of the solids, liquids and gases you can see.

Water freezes and turns into ice. Water boils and becomes steam. If you melt ice, the water comes back just as it was before. If you collect steam and let it cool down you have water again. Try heating and cooling water – with an adult's help – and see how it changes.

Why do these things happen? Water is made of tiny parts called **molecules.** They are much too small to see, even with a microscope. The water in a glass may look still, but all the molecules are moving. Imagine it like this:

When you cool water the molecules become colder. They huddle together, and finally stop moving about altogether. When this happens ice forms. When you heat up the water, the molecules become very excited. They rush about and bump into each other. They move so fast that they take off and spread around the room. The water has become a gas – steam. It is hard to keep a gas in one place because the molecules try to escape!

WATER MYTHS

BELOW **The Inuit used to believe that an animal allowed itself to be killed, but only if people pleased the animal's spirit. A wooden whale tied to the boat was supposed to bring luck in hunting whales.**

A myth is an ancient story about gods and strange happenings. A myth may try to explain things that happened long ago. Some myths have been passed down from generation to generation for centuries. Here is a myth about water.

Atlantis was an island. The people on Atlantis had big cities, plenty of gold and great parties. But most people were also very wicked. God decided to drown the wicked people. He warned everyone and gave them time to build ships and escape. Most of them did not pay attention.

God caused a huge storm. There were enormous waves and fierce storms. It rained for many weeks. Eventually the island sank into the sea. The good people escaped to tell their story.

This myth is known all around the world. People in South America and Africa have a flood story. Jews and Christians remember the great flood as the tale of Noah's Ark.

Write a modern story about a monster or a strange event to do with water.

OPPOSITE **When the dove returned to Noah with a branch in its beak, Noah knew the flood would soon be over.**

DIRTY WATER

People have always used water for washing. This makes the water dirty. Most types of natural dirt are **biodegradable**. The dirt is broken down by small animals and plants that live in the water.

In the past there were fewer people. They did not have washing powder and other things containing strong chemicals. All the dirt in the water was broken down until it was harmless.

Many modern chemicals are not biodegradable. When they enter the rivers, lakes and seas of the world they cause **pollution**. These pictures show how some chemicals get into water. Can you see why each chemical is dangerous?

1. Nuclear waste pumps out of this power station. The **radioactive waste** spreads into the sea. Plants, fish and other animals which live in the sea are poisoned.

2. Crude oil spills out of an oil tanker that has crashed. The oil floats on top of the water. The birds get covered in oil and they cannot fly. Fish can't breathe because no air can enter the water.

3. Sewage from household sewers pours into this river. All the washing-up liquid and detergent makes foam. The foam mounts up and **suffocates** the wildlife. The foam blows on to farms and houses.

Try to find out more about water pollution. How could it be prevented? Ask people to stop using dangerous chemicals. What else can they do to help keep water clean?

ACTIVITIES

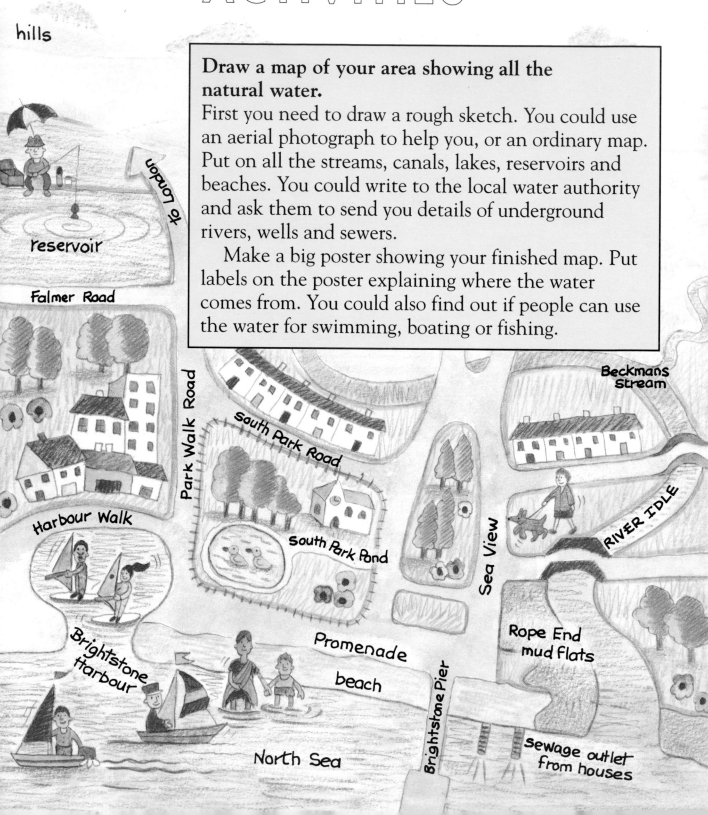

Draw a map of your area showing all the natural water.

First you need to draw a rough sketch. You could use an aerial photograph to help you, or an ordinary map. Put on all the streams, canals, lakes, reservoirs and beaches. You could write to the local water authority and ask them to send you details of underground rivers, wells and sewers.

Make a big poster showing your finished map. Put labels on the poster explaining where the water comes from. You could also find out if people can use the water for swimming, boating or fishing.

hills

reservoir

to London

Falmer Road

Park Walk Road

South Park Road

Beckmans Stream

RIVER IDLE

Sea View

Harbour Walk

South Park Pond

Brightstone Harbour

Rope End mud flats

Promenade

beach

Brightstone Pier

North Sea

sewage outlet from houses

Make a water-clock.

Ask an adult to help you with this activity.

1. Cut a large plastic bottle in half.
2. Make a hole in the cap with a pin, using a hammer.
3. Turn the top half of the bottle (A) upside-down and balance it in the bottom half of the bottle (B).
4. Fill A with water. The water drips down into B.
5. After one hour, make a mark on B to show where the water has reached. Make another mark each hour until all the water has gone through the cap.
6. Now empty B. Refill your water-clock with water to time how long various activities take, using the measurements you have made.

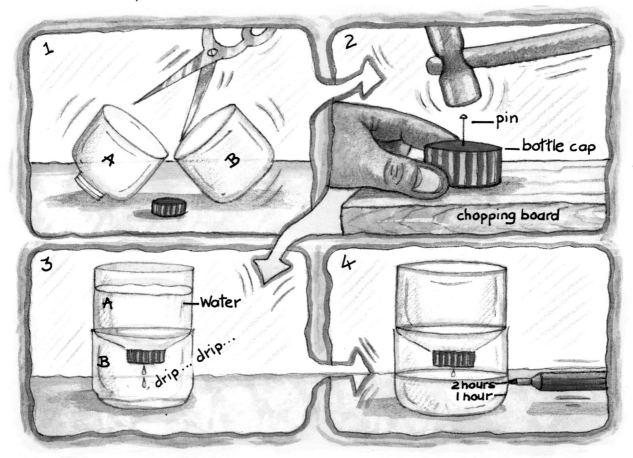

GLOSSARY

Aerobic exercise Exercise in which you use and need more air.

Aquifers Rocks under the ground which have tiny spaces that contain water.

Baptize To sprinkle someone with water, or put them under water, to show they are accepted as a member of the Church.

Biodegradable Able to rot away naturally.

Evaporates Turns from a liquid into a gas.

Hydroelectric power The electricity made when water turns a turbine.

Hydrotherapy Treatment using water to help move parts of your body that are stiff, or to strengthen weak muscles.

Inuit One of the original peoples of Canada and Greenland.

Molecules The tiny particles that substances are made up of.

Pollution Damage to the environment caused by waste materials.

Prediction What you think is going to happen.

Radioactive waste The harmful substances produced when nuclear fuel is used.

Reservoir A place where water is stored.

Spindle A part of a machine which turns round or on which something turns.

Suffocate To kill by stopping from breathing.

Turbine A machine with blades that are turned round by air, steam or water passing through them.

FINDING OUT MORE

Books
Catching the Light: Language in the Environment (Worldwide Fund for Nature, 1991)
Noah and his Ark by C. Storr (Franklin Watts, 1984)
Oceans and Seas by Terry Jennings (Oxford University Press, 1988)
Religions and *The Sea*, in *My First Library* series (Macdonald, 1987)
Water by Brenda Walpole (A & C Black, 1988)

Computer software
Into the Unknown : a Fifteenth-Century Voyage of Discovery
by Tressell Publications, 70 Grand Parade, Brighton BN2 2JA.
Water Mill by Chalksoft Ltd, PO Box 49, Spalding, Lincs PE11 1NZ.

Music
Fingal's Cave (The Hebrides) by F. Mendelssohn
Water Music by G. Handel
Yellow Submarine by *The Beatles*

Poetry
A Calendar of Poems, ed. Wes Magee (Bell and Hyman, 1986)

Teachers' resources
Water (Junior Projects No. 45, Scholastic)
Water (Poetry for Projects, Scholastic)
Water Pollution (Junior Education, September 1986)

INDEX

Page numbers in **bold** indicate subjects shown in pictures, but not mentioned in the text on those pages.

Picture Acknowledgements
The publishers would like to thank the following for allowing their illustrations to be used in this book: Bridgeman Art Library 5, 16, 25; British Film Institute 11; D. Cumming 12; Ecoscene 15; Eye Ubiquitous (P. Seheult) 21(top); Greenpeace (D. Dorreboom) 26 (bottom); I. Lilly 9, 20; C. Osborne 18; Tony Stone Worldwide (B. Gibson) 4; Topham 7, 21 (bottom), 26 (top); Wayland Picture Library (J. Woodcock) 6, (J. Holmes) 13, (A. Blackburn) 17, 23, 28, 29; Werner Forman Archive 8, 24; ZEFA *cover*, 27.

SERIOUSLY SILLY

SCARY
FAIRY TALES

GHOSTYSHOCKS
and the THREE MUMMIES

ORCHARD BOOKS
338 Euston Road, London NW1 3BH
Orchard Books Australia
Level 17/207 Kent Street, Sydney, NSW 2000

First published in 2015 by Orchard Books

ISBN 978 1 40832 965 8

Text © Laurence Anholt 2015
Illustrations © Arthur Robins 2015

A CIP catalogue record for this book is available
from the British Library.

3 5 7 9 10 8 6 4 2
Printed in Great Britain

Orchard Books is a division of Hachette Children's Books,
an Hachette UK company.

www.hachette.co.uk

SERIOUSLY SILLY

SCARY
FAIRY TALES

GHOSTYSHOCKS
and the THREE MUMMIES

Laurence Anholt
& Arthur Robins

ORCHARD

www.anholt.co.uk

GOOD EVENING, LADIES AND
GENTLEMEN.
My name is
THE MAN WITHOUT A HEAD.

Of course I have a head really... it's just
that my head is removable. It makes it so
much easier to brush my teeth.

So, you like SCARY STORIES, do you? Well,
I warn you, the stories I am about to tell
are so TERRIFYING that grown men have
been known to do wee-wees in their panties.

This story is about a girl named
Ghostyshocks, who made the mistake of
MESSING WITH A MUMMY and got
herself all wound up.

There was once a girl named Ghostyshocks.

She lived with her mother and father and her
baby brother in a big tent in the shade of some
palm trees in the desert. The family were very
poor, but they had a lovely life.

Ghostyshocks could swim in the oasis, or make
sandcastles, or relax in her deckchair eating dates,
which were her favourite.

In fact, there was only one thing the children were NOT allowed to do.

"You must never, never, never ride a camel into the endless desert," said their father.

"That's right," said their mother. "You will certainly get lost and you might even die of thirst."

"Even worse than that," said their father, "you may end up near the pyramids and you know who lives there..."

"Who lives in the pyramids?" whispered Ghostyshocks.

"Don't even ask!" said her mother and father together.

So, Ghostyshocks stayed near the tent, eating dates and playing with her pet camel (he never took the hump).

One day, it was her mother's birthday. Ghostyshocks was too poor to buy a present, but she was a kind girl.

"You two go out for the day," she told her mother and father. "I'll stay here and look after my brother. Don't worry, I am quite grown up now."

"You won't ride your camel into the... you know..." said her mother.

"No. I won't go into the desert," said Ghostyshocks.

"And you won't go near the... you know..." said her father.

"No. I won't go near the pyramids," said Ghostyshocks.

So they all said goodbye and Ghostyshocks took out a storybook to read to her baby brother.

But her brother was being very naughty. He kept running in and out of the tent with his nappy dangling all around his fat little legs.

"Ghostyshocks, Ghostyshocks, my nappy has come undone," he squealed.

Ghostyshocks put a new nappy on her baby brother, then she had a little rest in the shade.

When she woke up, her brother had gone!

Ghostyshocks searched high and low, but she couldn't find him anywhere. "Oh dear!" squealed Ghostyshocks. "Whatever will I do?"

What else could she do, Fans of Fear? The one thing she had promised not to do. Ghostyshocks put a bottle of lemonade and some suncream in a bag, threw a saddle on her pet camel (he never took the hump) and set off into the endless desert.

"My poor baby brother," she said. "He will surely die in the hot sun."

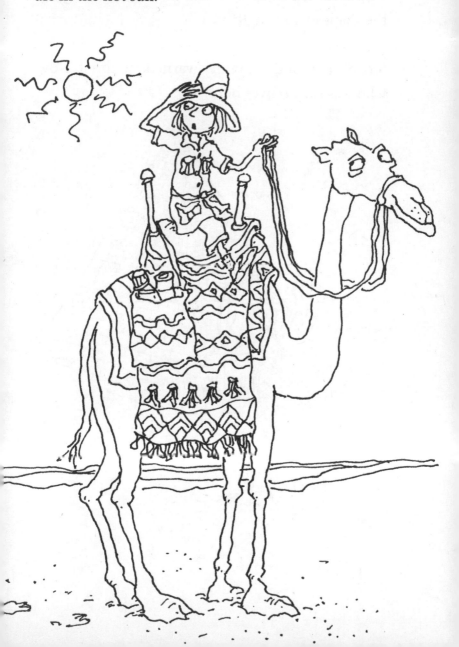

All day she rode and, as the sun went down, Ghostyshocks came to a strange stone building in the shape of a triangle.

"Oh dear," she wailed, "I hope this is not the terrible pyramid my father warned me about. Now who was it who lives here?"

Ghostyshocks tied up her pet camel (he never took the hump) and walked all around, but she couldn't find a door.

At last, she climbed right to the top of the pyramid. There was a strange stone carving with a picture of a man playing a trumpet.

It said 'This is the tomb of the king – Toot and Come In'.

Suddenly the tip of the pyramid flipped open. Ghostyshocks peered inside. She called for her baby brother, but there was no answer. She leaned over a bit further…

Suddenly, Ghostyshocks tumbled head over heels inside the cold, dark pyramid.

She landed with a bump in a triangular kitchen. On a stone table were three bowls. In the bowls were some juicy dates, and Ghostyshocks felt very, very hungry.

"I'll just try a few dates," she said. "I'm sure nobody will mind."

First, she tried the big bowl, but the dates were so big they didn't fit in her mouth.

Then she tried the middle-sized bowl, but the dates were too sweet and sticky.

Last of all, she tried the teeny-weeny baby bowl, and the dates were exactly right, so she ate every one and spat the stones in the bowl.

Ghostyshocks looked around. She saw some stone steps going deep down inside the pyramid. She felt very nervous, but she had to find her baby brother. It looked dark down there, but Ghostyshocks found a burning torch.

She tiptoed down the cold stone steps until she reached a spooky triangular room with weird paintings on the walls. But she couldn't find her baby brother.

Ghostyshocks was just about to run back up the stairs, when she noticed something amazing in a corner. She couldn't believe her eyes! There was a huge pile of shiny jewels, glittering bracelets, and golden necklaces.

"Oh!" said Ghostyshocks. "Treasure! I'll just put on one of those necklaces. Nobody will mind."

First, she tried on a big necklace, but that was so long it dragged on the floor.

Then she tried a middle-sized necklace, but that was so heavy she almost fell over.

Then she tried a teeny-weeny golden necklace and some teeny-weeny sparkling bracelets and they fitted perfectly.

Suddenly Ghostyshocks felt tired. She saw three nicely painted sarcophaguses with their lids open.

"I'll just have a little nap," she said, yawning. "Nobody will mind."

She put down the torch and climbed in the huge sarcophagus, but that was far too big.

Next, she climbed in the middle-sized sarcophagus, but that was far too soft.

Then she climbed in the teeny-weeny sarcophagus and that was exactly right. So she shut the lid and fell fast asleep, and dreamed about the endless desert.

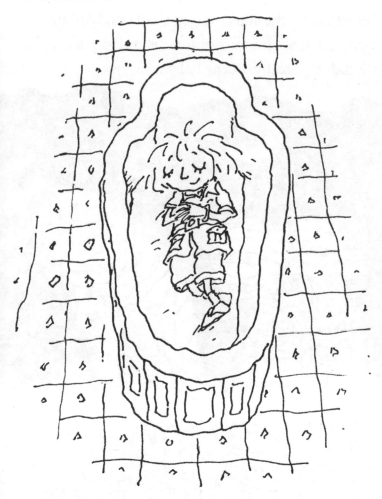

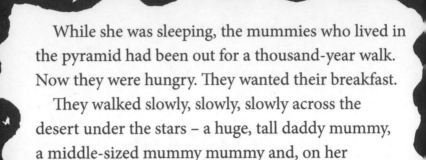

While she was sleeping, the mummies who lived in the pyramid had been out for a thousand-year walk. Now they were hungry. They wanted their breakfast.

They walked slowly, slowly, slowly across the desert under the stars – a huge, tall daddy mummy, a middle-sized mummy mummy and, on her shoulders, a teeny-weeny baby mummy.

The three mummies climbed slowly, slowly, slowly into the pyramid. They looked at all the date stones on the kitchen floor.

"SOMEONE'S BEEN EATING MY DATES!" roared the huge, tall daddy mummy.

"SOMEONE'S BEEN EATING MY DATES!" groaned the middle-sized mummy mummy.

But the teeny-weeny baby mummy was wrapped up so tight, that all he could do was point and say,

Then the three mummies walked slowly, slowly, slowly down the cold stone steps.

"SOMEONE'S BEEN PLAYING WITH MY JEWELS!" roared the huge, tall daddy mummy.

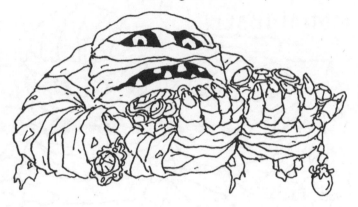

"SOMEONE'S BEEN PLAYING WITH MY JEWELS!" groaned the middle-sized mummy mummy.

But the teeny weeny baby mummy was wrapped
up so tight, that all he could do was point and say,

Then the three mummies walked slowly, slowly, slowly towards the sarcophaguses.

"SOMEONE'S BEEN SLEEPING IN MY SARCOPHAGUS!" roared the huge, tall daddy mummy.

"SOMEONE'S BEEN SLEEPING IN MY SARCOPHAGUS!" groaned the middle-sized mummy mummy.

But the teeny-weeny baby mummy was wrapped up so tight, that all he could do was point at the little sarcophagus and say,

Just then, Ghostyshocks woke up. She pushed
open the lid and saw the three mummies –

"EEEEEEEEEEEEEE EEEEEEEEEEEEEEEE EEEEEK!!!!"

she screamed. "I WANT MY MUMMY!"

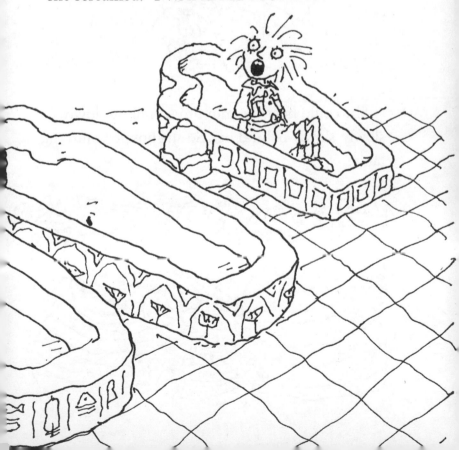

The three mummies walked towards her, slowly, slowly, slowly. Ghostyshocks hopped out of the sarcophagus and ran up the cold stone steps into the kitchen. She looked up at the door, but it was far too high for her to reach.

She could hear the mummies coming slowly, slowly, slowly behind her. So she hopped onto the table.

Suddenly, the teeny weeny baby mummy came running into the kitchen. His bandages were dangling all around his fat little legs.

"EEEEEEEEEEEEEEEEEEEEEEEK!!!!"

screamed Ghostyshocks. "I want my mummy!"

"Ghostyshocks, Ghostyshocks, my nappy has come undone," said the teeny-weeny baby.

Have you guessed, Fans of Fear? It was not a teeny-weeny baby mummy. How could you think such a foolish thing? No this was Ghostyshocks' naughty little baby brother.

You see, the huge, tall daddy mummy and
the middle sized mummy mummy had been
walking in the endless desert when they found
Ghostyshocks' baby brother out on his own, with
his nappy dangling all around his fat little legs.

They loved babies and had wanted one for
thousands of years. Of course, they didn't want
him to get burnt by the hot sun, so they wrapped
him up nice and tight in bandages and carried
him slowly, slowly, slowly back to their nice
cold pyramid.

And now the two mummies were coming slowly, slowly, slowly up the stairs and they were very, very angry. They were angry because someone had taken their dates and they were even angrier because someone had helped herself to their lovely glittering bracelets and jewels and most of all, Fans of Fear, the mummies were furious because someone had been sleeping in their sarcophagus.

The daddy mummy and the mummy mummy came slowly, slowly, slowly into the triangular kitchen. They reached our their horrible bandaged hands, when, quick as a flash, Ghostyshocks picked up her little brother, lifted him up and pushed him through the lid of the pyramid.

The big, tall daddy mummy stretched out to grab her, but just then, Ghostyshocks saw the long bandage dangling from above. She climbed up as quickly as she could and slammed the lid of the pyramid.

Then Ghostyshocks and her baby brother, hopped onto her pet camel (he never took the hump) and galloped back across the desert as fast as they could go.

When their mother and father came back from their birthday outing, they found Ghostyshocks and her baby brother, lying peacefully in a deckchair finishing their storybook.

You see, Fans of Fear, after a long night with the mummies, it was time to relax and unwind. You could say the children were wrapped up in a story.

And that was the terrifying tale of **GHOSTYSHOCKS** and the **THREE MUMMIES.** Of course, every word was true. Goodnight, Fans of Fear – and if you go out tonight, remember to wrap up well!

SERIOUSLY SILLY

SCARY
FAIRY TALES

LAURENCE ANHOLT & ARTHUR ROBINS

COLLECT THEM ALL!

Also available
as an ebook